S0-AUA-004

VENUS
ON THE
FRINGE

**Creating a
Short Game
That Works
for Humans!**

Introducing the "V" Factor

Debbie Steinbach

Foreword by Jan Stephenson,
winner of 16 L.P.G.A. events,
including 3 major championships

PRO
P
PROMOTIONS

Library of Congress Cataloging-in-Publication Data

Steinbach, Debbie.
     Venus on the Fringe :Creating a Short Game That Works for Humans.
Introducing the "V Factor" / Debbie Steinbach ; foreword by Jan Stephenson.

       p.   cm.
     ISBN 0-9749308-0-6
     1. Golf for women.

 PRO PROMOTIONS

Copyright © 2004 by Venus Golf, LLC. All rights reserved. Printed in the United States of America. Except as permitted under the United States Copyright Act of 1976, no part of this publication may be reproduced or distributed in any form or by any means, or stored in a database or retrieval system, without the prior written permission of the publisher.

Venus Golf, Venus View, Y Factor, V Factor, Venus Character Girl and The Money Club are all Registered Trademarks of Venus Golf, LLC

ISBN 0-9749308-0-6

This book is set in Weiss
Printed and bound by AdMedia, Palm Springs, CA

Cover design by Digital Overture

Cover Photo by Joann Dost
Interior photographs by Scott Avra and Bill Park

Pro Promotions books are available at special quantity discounts to use as premiums and sales promotions, or for use in corporate training programs. For more information, please write to the Director of Special Sales, Pro Promotions, 78-110 Calle Norte, La Quinta, CA 92253, call 888.678.3687, or contact your local bookstore.

To be or not to be, that is the question.
SHAKESPEARE - AUTHOR, MALE

To **V** or not to **V**, that is the question.
STEINBACH - AUTHOR, FEMALE

CONTENTS

Part I: Ground Shots

Putting   3

Rolling a ball into a hole should be simple. But like life, putting tends to get unnecessarily complicated. In Part 1, Venus simplifies the mystical and explains the reality of putting starting with her Linear Light Bulb Moment. From that point, she gets down to business and makes the learning process simple.

Chipping   67

Venus continues to keep the information super simple with this very important – not complex – part of the game. She breaks it down into golfer-friendly topics including: Show Me the Money; Decisions, Decisions; Making Magic; Back to Basics; Give Me Another "V"; Getting a Grip to Chip; Posture Perfect; Anchor Yourself; Ball Position; Square the Clubface; Swing Path; The Rhythm Method for Chipping; Finish What You've Started; and Taylor's Question.

Part II: Air Shots

1. The Venus Pitch   89

Now that you're on a roll, it's time to get the ball in the air and land it close enough to the hole to make putting even easier. In this section Venus covers: The Basic Golf Grip; Taking a Stance; Posture; Give Me a "Y"; Visualization; Getting Started; Backswing in Motion; Pitching for Dollars; Following Through; Smoothing Out Those Ups and Downs; Hit and Stop; and finally, Shank You Very Much.

2. How to be a Sand Shark   109

The average golfer not only has a fear of water, but also an unnatural fear of sand. Venus takes the fear out of going to the beach, as she takes you through: Lob or Sand Wedge; The Sound of Music; Start with a Weak Grip; Open Stance; Go Outside to Get In; Open for Business; Ball Position; Room for Error; Going to the Cleaners — Spin and Fold; The Short and Long of It; Fried Eggs; Lies, Lies and More Lies; and A Positive Spin

3. Mastering the Lob Shot 127

We've all heard about the "Lob" shot, and have probably heard even more about how hard and even dangerous it can be. Venus eliminates the fear and keeps it simple in these easy to understand steps: Taking the Gamble; Open Sesame; Grip of the "Weak"; Sandra on Ball Position; Backswing in Motion; Back to the Cleaners; and you must remember to Pose for the Cameras.

Part III: Short Game Drills for Better Skills

To reinforce everything you've learned in Parts I and II, Venus has put together a series of short game drills for you to use in your practice sessions. They are simple, fun and will really help your short game.

1. Putting 137

Tennis Ball Drill; The Venus 2-Ball Putting Drill; Eyes Wide Shut Drill; Eyes on the Hole Drill; Two Club Drill; Putt on Down the Line Drill; Drinking Glass Drill; Against a Board Drill; Under the String Drill; Metronome Drill

2. Chipping 145

Get a Line Drill; Chip to a Coin Drill; Three-Foot Circle Drill

3. Pitching 147

Underhand Toss Drill; One-Arm Drill; Club on the Green Drill

4. Sand 149

Into the Bucket Drill; Drawing a Line in the Sand Drill; Tee It Up Drill

5. Lob 151

Back to the Bucket Drill; Up and Over Drill; Over the Bunker Drill

The "Fun Factor" 154

Afterword 157

Venus Values 159

FOREWORD

I am so happy that Debbie's first book, *Venus on the Fairway*, is so successful. Having competed on the LPGA Tour for 30 years, playing in pro-ams and being involved with teaching women, it was great to see someone finally discussing the differences between men and women when it comes to golf instruction.

I thought her book was so good that I couldn't wait to see what she would come out with next. Lo and behold, I got a phone call from Debbie. She told me that her first book went great (which I already knew), and she was going to write a new one on the short game. I asked her if there was any way that I could help, and she said; "How about you writing the forward?" So here I am.

I've never written a forward before, although I have been too forward (with my statements) just about my whole career. I figure this is just one more way I can get to say what I believe. And let me tell you something, I KNOW YOU WILL LOVE THIS BOOK!

This new book on the short game is even more enlightening than Debbie's first one. As a junior golfer in Australia, I had to rely on the raw ideas of my father, because at that time there was very little emphasis on short game instruction. We worked every day on shots from 60 yards and in, as well as chipping and making four-foot putts.

My father always emphasized that in order to win you must have a great short game. You have to make the short putts for birdies, and you must be able to get up and down. In tournaments, the short game is the key to not dropping shots and losing one to the field. You can hit it to eight feet all day, but if you can't finish, you can't score and you can't win.

In 1981 I had three LPGA wins including my first Major and two international wins. To give you an idea of how I did it, that year I was named Short Game Player of the Year on the LPGA Tour.

Needless to say, I believe in the importance of the short game. Debbie's refreshing and educational approach to teaching in *Venus on the Fringe* is long overdue.

We have been friends for 25 years and I always felt that she was one of those players who did not get everything she should have from her game and talent. But now, through her teaching and ability to communicate, Debbie is achieving everything she has always deserved as a professional.

Can you believe it? A golf superstar at long last! And believe me, this book is so good that I can't wait to read her next one.

Jan Stephenson

ACKNOWLEDGMENTS

This is my opportunity to thank those who have played a role in my writing *Venus On The Fringe*.

Starting with the first member of the Venus Golf Team, Steve Adams, I thank you for being my "Rock Of Gibraltar." Everybody needs someone who believes in them and supports them through thick and thin. You have been that person for me.

Susan McCallum, "my right arm." A heart felt thanks for your never-ending hard work, friendship, and enthusiasm for this and every project we take on. You have proven to be the ultimate team player.

Ray Scarpa, "The OZ," I am so very grateful to have you working your magic and making business sense out of everything I throw at you. Just knowing you are behind that curtain gives me the   confidence to keep plugging along. You are more than a friend, you are a "find!"

Speaking of finds, Courtney Capdeville, was invaluable as the art director. She told me early on that she enjoyed this particular   project and it is clear that Courtney has the Venus Vision!

Of course there were other finds too, such as Joann Dost who shot the cover for the front of the book. Joann and I have been friends since our LPGA playing days. She is now an award winning golf photographer, and Joann graciously took the cover shot not only as a favor to Venus, but also to help promote the awareness of breast cancer, of which Joann is a survivor.

When Joann left town, Scott Avra took over with the photos. It took 6 hours of shooting, and when he finished, we had five minutes to spare as the sun went completely down behind the palm trees!

Finally, when last-minute pick-up shots were needed, Bill Park was called into action. Bill did more than just take pick-up shots, he also edited and added graphics to many of the pictures on his home computer. We now call him "Mr. Clutch!"

Many friends came through for me in the clutch. Three of them come to mind instantly, Arnold Palmer, Jan Stephenson, and Sandra Post. All three never hesitated when I asked for their support and endorsements.

Friends are a wonderful gift. Parker Smith called me out of the blue this past summer and invited me to a publishers conference on the beautiful island of Aruba. Thanks to this great opportunity I was able to escape my life in the desert and throw myself into writing.

Aruba not only inspired me to write again, but that is where I met Hal Quinn, who became my editor. Hal is an 8 handicap from Canada, so it was fate that we met during the publisher's conference. You did a great job Hal!

As I have stated earlier, this book has been a team effort and I could write something about everyone. Of course if I did, this acknowledgment would be longer than the book itself. So let me introduce my "supporting cast" of friends, mentors, and role models.

Starting with my "chief proof reader," Marcia Hoyt, Susan Pappas, Alan Newman, Pat Norton, Jane Dally, Jan Harrington, Burch Riber, Carol McCloskey-Delich, Pam Swensen, Penny Lawton, Kathy Bissell, Donna Craig, Jack McCallum, JoAnn Hoffman, Marcy Smothers, Clare Sante, Andy Brumer, Bill Wiles, Katie Storer, Kathy Le, Patty Lynn, Joyce Loiseau, Ed Hise, Judy Furst, Carol Hogan, Kerri Clark, Terry Cronin, Gayle Triolo, Nancy Saunders, Renee Cox, Greg Houlgate, Dr. Maxann Shwartz, Dr. Bob Spaan, Dr. Craig Farnsworth, Dr. Bruce Ogilvie, Dr. Rome Hanning, Dr. Frank Crinella, John Cahoon, Dr. Tom Costa, Marian Whiteman, Marj Dusay, Jane Hopkins, Tom Bennison, Sherry Binger, Cheryl Dixon, Mike Jamison, Pat Mateer, Patrice Hutin, Cynthia Lester, Paul and Karen Sullivan, Bentley Renker, Susan Bryck, Nancy Charney, Robyn Stowell, Debbie Waitkus, J.D. Ebersberger, David Chapman, Donna Long, Taylor Manning, Barbara Thompson, and my loyal sisters Claudia Tynan and Cynthia Mezenski, along with my mom, Millie Brandstetter and dad, Carl Meisterlin. (If I left anyone out, I will catch you in the next book!)

XI

I would also like to thank the various golf organizations that have been so very supportive of Venus and her dreams.

EWGA - Executive Women's Golf Association
WIGI - Women In The Golf Industry
WSCGA - Women's Southern California Golf Association
MILO - Meeting Industry Ladies Organization
LPGA - Ladies Professional Golf Association
ING - International Network of Golf
Women's Sunriver Golf Forum
Ladies Fore Golf
JuniorGolfing.com

Rally For A Cure®, the nation's largest cause-oriented women's golf program, supports the Susan G. Komen Breast Cancer Foundation. As the "Official Golf Spokesperson," Venus continues to endorse, promote and support Rally For A Cure®.

And finally I would like to thank all my students past and present who inspire and challenge me to continue growing and learning every day. This book may be finished, but Venus Golf has only just begun!

Venus

INTRODUCTION

Allow me to introduce myself. My name is Debbie Steinbach, also known as "Venus" since my first book, Venus On The Fairway was published in 2001, written with friend and author Kathleen Bissell.

Before becoming an author and teaching pro, or coach as I like to be called, I competed on the LPGA Tour for 11 years. In that time I was more than humbled by players with incredible short games.

For example, I'll never forget being paired with Nancy Lopez in the Lady Keystone event in Hershey, Pennsylvania, back in the days when her husband, major league baseball player Ray Knight, was caddying for her.

Nancy was not hitting her driver well that particular day, hitting only five or six fairways. She hit even fewer greens in regulation.

I, on the other hand, was having a great day with regards to my ball striking, hitting every fairway and every green. While I may have been hitting the ball like a machine, Nancy was getting the ball into the hole like a magician.

She chipped in twice, sank a sand shot from a greenside bunker, and pitched it in from 40 yards off the green. Nancy's putting stroke was so smooth you just knew she was going to make every putt, and she did. When Nancy signed her scorecard it was for a 68!

Meanwhile, after 18 long walks with my putter, I signed mine for a disappointing 72, even par. Nancy had clearly beaten me with her short game.

I looked like I was playing like a champ, but had not "closed the deal." Nancy took care of business and moved up in the standings to play with the leaders the next day while I stayed right where I started, in the middle of the pack. That was my "light bulb" moment on how a reliable short game will "close the deal."

I immediately concentrated on improving my short game. That

journey lead me too a deep appreciation of the masters of the short game, including legends such as Johnny Revolta, Ernie Vossler, and the great Paul Runyan, from whom I learned so much. The result was a love, respect, and understanding of the short game that I want to pass onto you.

Since the publication of the first book, Venus On The Fairway, I am often asked why I did not include the shorter swings. It's a good question, given the valuable lessons I have learned while competing on the LPGA Tour.

My answer is that the first book was written to deal with the differences between men and women as they apply to the full swing. Other than the obvious strength factor, I don't see any differences between men and women when it comes to the short game. The technique is the same for everyone.

I also wanted to write a separate book on the short game because I want to avoid a dangerous golfing virus I call "TMI" — too much information. Keeping the learning process simple is what the Venus method is all about.

I recognize that you are not a human computer, but a human being. Therefore, as I introduce various aspects of the short game technique, I promise to feed you information that is simple and easy to digest. Starting with this tasty bit of the **Venus View** on golf.

Venus View: *Putting and chipping are played along the ground; all other golf shots are played in the air.*

It can't get any simpler than that, so let's get started...........

XVI

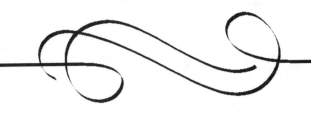

PART 1

GROUND SHOTS

Putting & Chipping

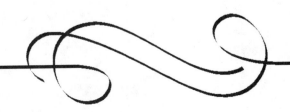

MY LINEAR 'LIGHT BULB' MOMENT

I didn't just wake up one morning with the realization that putting is a linear stroke. The "light bulb" turned on one rainy night in Georgia back in the late 1970s. I was playing on the LPGA Tour and was not exactly at the top of the money list. I decided to visit my friend Jan Stephenson – who just happens to have won 16 LPGA titles, including three Majors – in her hotel room. Jan was always good for some honest words of wisdom and I needed a large dose.

When I entered the room, I knew we would not be reading the tarot cards! Jan had this training aid called a Putting Track set up right in the middle of the room. It had been designed by Dave Pelz and Jan was rolling ball after ball through the middle of this contraption.

She was focusing on stroking the ball while not letting her putter head touch the railings on each side of the track. Keeping the putter head between the rails kept it square to the target line. She was training her putting stroke to move directly back and through on a straight line, thus her club path was linear — a straight line.

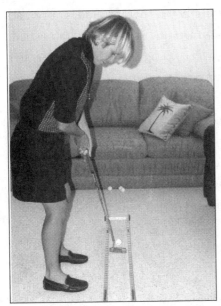

Venus practicing with her own putting track to groove a linear stroke.

I told Jan that I thought this was an unnatural stroke, because the putter head should move a little inside on the back swing, and then back to inside on the follow through.

I told her I believed all golf shots were played out away from the body, including the putting stroke, and therefore the putting stroke should be on more of a curve. A linear club path — a straight line — just didn't look natural to me.

Jan gave me a look of disbelief that I will never forget! She must have thought I had some nerve telling her the secret of putting, considering what a lousy putter I was and what a great putter she was. Fortunately for me, she didn't kick me out of the room. Instead she gave me that dose of wisdom I'd come looking for.

Jan told me about working with Dave Pelz (back then a relative unknown, but now acknowledged as a guru of the short game) and that he had given her the Putting Track to help her swing the putter in a more pendulum-like fashion.

4

As I watched her stroke ball after ball, I noticed how her elbows pointed outwards. I could see that the shape of her elbows resembled the letter "V" and the "V" was swinging back and then forward while maintaining the "V" shape.

Jan looked as though she was using her elbows as guides. She had turned herself into a human putting machine stroking ball after ball, end over end, perfectly. The balls were lining up against each other across the room. I was sold. Linear it was!

Whether you are using a standard putter, a belly putter, a long putter or a short putter, the goal is to sweep the club head on as linear (straight) a path as possible — straight back and straight through.

I don't need years of research and statistics to prove to me that this is indeed the best method of putting. Jan proved it back in the 70s & 80's and now my students prove it to me every day!

2

CHOOSE YOUR WEAPON

My Father has used just one putter for as long as I can remember. It's an old blade style model with a heel that curls up like a ram's horn. Dad is convinced that this crazy antique is superior to anything on the planet. He's married to it and they have had a long and wonderful marriage.

When Nancy Lopez was winning every tournament in sight, she used a mallet head putter. Nancy was so convinced it was lucky that she would not tempt fate by re-gripping it – even after the grip had turned completely crooked and was no longer even set square to the shaft. It didn't matter; she'd just point her finger down that old worn grip and proceed to put a perfect roll on the ball, time after time.

Dad and Nancy loved those putters and were so successful with them – albeit, not on quite the same plane – because as in any good relationship, it was based on an overriding confidence.

That's what you're looking for in a putter, a club that makes you feel confident. It's a very personal choice.

The most important factor in choosing a putter is to pick one you like. In other words, you must have positive vibes about your putter. It is your magic wand, so to speak, so you must choose very carefully.

Think of yourself as Harry Potter and select the magic wand that looks and feels good to you.

The only Venus advice on putters is to remember that you want to choose a putter that will help you to comfortably address the ball and encourage a back and forward pendulum-like motion.

You have the choice of a long putter, belly putter, or standard length putter.

*Standard Putter
(for those who
like vanilla)*

Belly Putter (works best when not pregnant)

Long Putter (for those who think big!)

3

GET A GRIP

Your putting grip is different from the grip you use for full swing shots. The full swing grip must allow the wrists to break – hinge – while the putting grip is designed to keep the wrists very quiet throughout the stroke (hinging only on the longest putts).

11

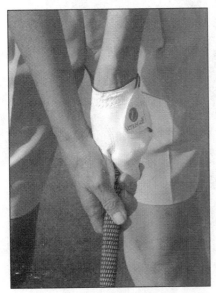

Full swing grip: For hand rotation and hinging action.

Putting grip: For quiet hands and no hinging action.

There are endless variations, but the three basic putting grips are:

The 10-finger grip: Both hands are on the club with the fingers more under the handle than with the grip used for the full swing. Both thumbs are placed directly down the top of the line of the putter shaft.

This is a good grip for beginners. It's also a great way to feel connected to the club because all of your fingers are on it and the back of the lead hand is facing the target line. The hands oppose each other so that neither hand works more than the other.

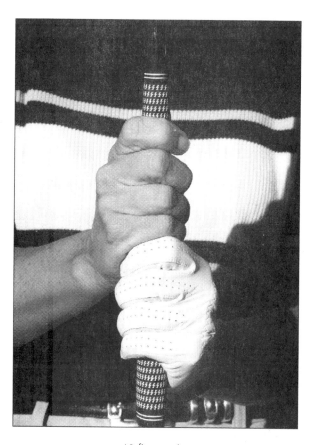

10 finger grip.

The reverse overlap grip: This is the most popular grip among the touring pros on both the LPGA and the PGA Tours. It's very similar to the ten finger grip except that the forefinger of the lower hand is placed over the index finger of the top hand. The entire lead hand is on the handle plus the three fingers and the thumb of the top hand.

The fingers on both hands are positioned more under the handle than the standard golf grip which allows them to oppose each other with the back of the lead hand facing the target line.

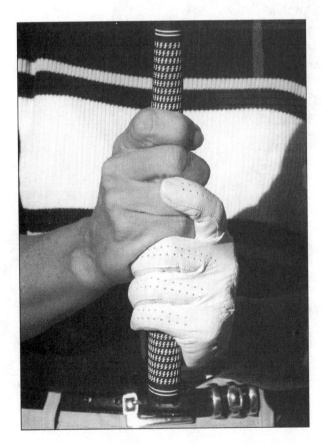

Reverse overlap grip.

13

The lead hand low grip: This is my personal favorite because placing the lead hand below the other hand eliminates any use of the wrists during the stroke. This grip keeps the lead wrist rigid while making it harder for the back hand to take over and cause the wrists to hinge. And it allows the shoulders to set up in a level position at address which helps to keep the clubhead moving low to the ground.

If you can get comfortable with the lead hand low grip, this is the one I recommend.

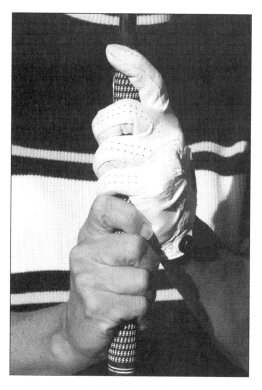

Lead hand low grip.

Promotes level shoulders.

Get in Touch with Your "Feelings"

Experiment with grip pressure as well. This will be different for everyone, yet grip pressure is a major factor in successful putting. Whether you hold the club firmly or with "soft" hands, keeping your grip pressure constant is key to being a good putter.

This may sound easy enough, but it's not. Grip pressure is an acquired feeling. But how does one teach a feeling? My answer is to introduce "The V Factor!"

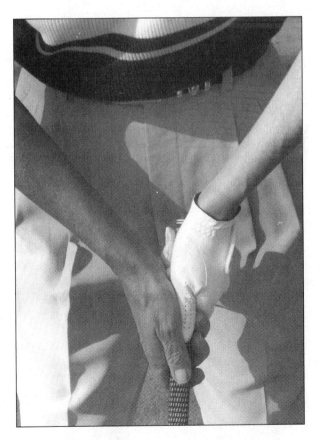

On a scale of 1 to 5, my grip pressure is a 5.

INTRODUCING
THE "V FACTOR"

As Jan Stephenson demonstrated, the best method for consistent and accurate putting is a linear stroke. The easiest way to create that consistently straight pendulum putting motion (the linear stroke) is to employ the "V Factor."

The "V" in the "V Factor" refers to the letter V-like shape formed by the elbows, lower arms and hands when a golfer is positioned correctly over a putt at address.

One of the major challenges of putting is preventing the wrists

17

Give me a "V."

from breaking – hinging – during the stroke. The "V Factor" not only promotes an ideal linear stoke but minimizes wrist hinging by focusing the feeling of the putting motion where it belongs – in the big muscles of the shoulders and upper arms, not in the wrists and lower arms.

The distance between the elbows remains constant throughout the putting stroke.

Some golfers like to create a wide V, others a narrow V. (When I first started employing the "V Factor," I imagined I had a basketball between my elbows).

"Air" Venus.

It doesn't matter how wide or narrow your personal V is as long as your address position creates the V shape and you maintain the V throughout the stroke.

By swinging the V back and forth in one piece with the arms and

Wide V.   *Narrow V.*

19

shoulders working together as a single unit, you'll create a linear and consistent stroke and the V will become a major factor in your game.

Maintain the "V" on both the back swing and follow through.

5

GET SET
TO GO

Comfort Zone

Your putting posture has to be correct to support the "V Factor" set up and linear swing path. This is where you need to set up for success.

Tilt from the waist so that the arms and hands hang directly below the shoulder line and your eyes are positioned directly over the ball.

Notice how eyes are directly over the ball.

You may want to actually drop a ball from your eye line to check your head position.

You should feel stable and balanced, and in fact, down right comfortable. To make sure you are stable and balanced, ask someone to give you the "Venus Push Test." Have them push you in any direction, and see if you can remain balanced.

I only let my best friends "push" me around!

Anchors away

At address, "anchor" your weight slightly onto your lead side so you won't be tempted to shift or move during your stroke. Too often we not only move our heads when we putt, but we actually move our whole bodies.

I used to watch the great Kathy Whitworth anchor herself all the time when she putted. Not surprisingly, she was the most consistent putter I ever played golf with. In fact, she won a record 88 LPGA tournaments, so she definitely knew a thing or two about anchoring!

To get yourself anchored, lean slightly onto your lead heal until you feel like your weight is locked in and grounded.

This anchoring position helps create a "forward press," a key to good putting. It shifts your grip and your body slightly toward the target positioning your hands slightly in front of the ball at address, or, pressed forward.

23

Notice how I am anchored with my hands forward of ball.

Stance and Ball Position

The width of your stance is completely up to you. I personally don't take a wide stance because putting is not a stroke that requires any weight shift or extra power. Experiment to find the width of stance that feels comfortable to you.

When it comes to ball position, I have a more definite opinion because it's very important to put an end-over-end roll on the golf ball to putt consistently.

Venus believes that the key to an end-over-end roll is to position the ball slightly forward of center in your stance. This will give you the best chance of making contact squarely at the equator of the ball to impart the proper roll. When the ball is struck below the equator it can skid and go off line.

Ball positioned too far back　　*Correct ball positioned slightly forward of center.*

6

STROKE OF GENIUS

Imagine

The best and most effective visualization for a linear putting stroke is a pendulum. Picture in your mind the putter head literally swinging back and forth on a linear path like a pendulum in a big old clock, swinging back at the same speed that it swings forward.

"tick"

"tock"

The Rhythm Method

Rhythm is critical to a good repeating stroke.

Without good rhythm, you won't be able to put a smooth roll on the ball.

I like to practice the rhythm method of putting by actually saying "tick" on the back swing and a slightly louder "tock" on the follow through. I say the "tock" louder to make sure I don't decelerate on the forward swing.

I know a lot of good putters who just count "one" on the back swing and "two" on the follow through. It doesn't really matter what you say to yourself as long as you ingrain in your brain that the head of the putter must swing back and forth in a rhythmic manner.

One way to practice a more consistent rhythm is to use a metronome.

There are metronomes available today that you attach to the brim of your visor or hat so you're the only one to hear the beeps. This way, you can practice all you want and nobody even knows what you're doing. They'll see you have great rhythm, but they won't hear why!

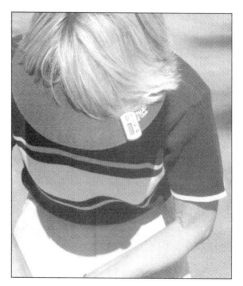

Not as good as Kenny G., but still has rhythm.

Rock The Baby

Rocking the shoulders back and forth as they rotate under the head creates the pendulum motion. To get the feeling of the correct pendulum motion, set up in your "V Factor" position and imagine that you have a small child in your arms. Now just "rock the baby" and feel how your shoulders move back and forth under your head in a very smooth and rhythmic way.

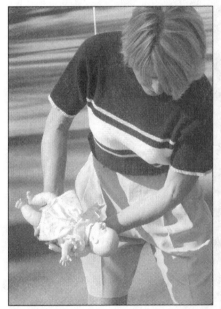 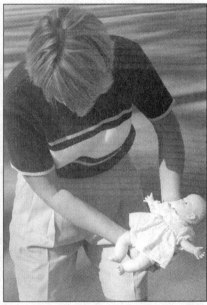

Disclaimer: Any resemblance to a real baby is purely coincidental. No letters, please!

Accelerate To Celebrate

A true pendulum will swing at the same speed in both directions and the same distance back and forward.

It is important that the distance the putter travels on the back stroke be the same as the distance it travels on the follow through. It's equally important that the follow through continues down the target line after putting the ball. It is crucial to continue that momentum through the ball at impact; otherwise your putt will be short and will go off line.

Make sure you accelerate through to your finish position.

Rolling Along...

Any touring pro will tell you that keeping the putter head low to the ground throughout the stroke is fundamental to producing the ideal end-over-end roll on the ball.

In my first book, "Venus On The Fairway", I introduced a new visualization to golf regarding rolling the clubhead away from the ball on the takeaway. It works for the full swing and will also help you keep the putter head close to the ground when putting.

Imagine that there are a set of wheels on the bottom of the putter head. This visualization is especially good for putting as it's easy to imagine rolling the putter head away from the ball in a smooth and effortless manner and rolling it back the same way through the ball.

My junior students like this image so much that they've dubbed their imaginary wheels "roller blades." Think of the wheels and get your putts rolling along.

*The Venus version
of a "roller blade."*

Hold That Pose

You might not think so, but the finish position is just as important in putting as it is with the full swing.

When you hold the position of the putter head after you have completed your stroke, you get feedback on where the clubface is aimed and whether or not the ball has traveled down the intended line.

Train yourself to hold your finish. Mimic the professionals at their best. Pick your favorite pro and use them as a model. Focus on how they hold their finish.

If posing at the end of the putting stroke works for the best of the best, then it's certainly going to work for you. Follow the leaders and hold that pose!

Hold your finish to check path and clubface position.

7

BALL CONTACT

I cannot overemphasize how much striking the ball on the sweet spot of the putter affects the way the ball rolls, the direction it goes, and the distance it travels.

If I had a Hammer

I have a good friend, Dr. Bob Spaan, who has been working with me for years on coming up with answers about the mysterious art of putting. We always come back to the starting point — ball contact.

Dr. Bob is a genius who reminds me of the mad scientist in the movie, *Back to the Future*. I've nicknamed him "The Wiz," which is from another movie, but it suits him.

35

Dr. Bob, "The Wiz" and Venus.   *"The Wiz" making his point.*

The most creative putting aid "The Wiz" ever developed to teach solid ball contact is a club with a hammerhead replacing the putter head. His concept is to train the player to strike the golf ball solidly with the head of the hammer as though you are driving a nail directly into the back of the ball.

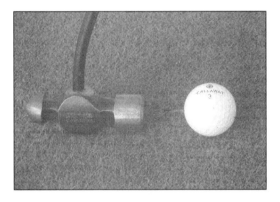

Stroke on the level of the ball, as though you are driving a nail into the center.

Although the use of a hammer is illegal for golf purposes, you do want to make the same solid contact on the sweet spot of your putter.

Most putters today have a line or an alignment feature marked on the top of the putter head to indicate the true center of the club. When lining up your putt, align the marking on the clubhead directly behind the center of the ball. Focus on that line or mark on the putter and strike the ball directly on its marking to guarantee solid contact.

Use the line to make solid contact.

36

After my first humbling session with the hammerhead, I remember handing it back to "The Wiz" and thanking him for the exercise. No doubt I needed my own ball contact to be more precise.

But "The Wiz" was not satisfied. He handed the hammerhead putter right back to me and said: "Okay, now hit putts with the other end of the hammer." Now, that's what I call precision putting!

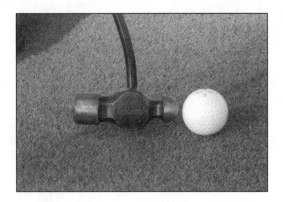

Have I made my point?

8

ALIGNMENT: GET ON DOWN THE LINE

Putting alignment is a three part process. Number one where you aim with your eyes, number two where you aim with your clubface, and number three where you aim your body.

The Eyes Have It-

I mentioned in *Venus On The Fairway* that it doesn't matter if you have the best swing in the world, if you are aiming to the right of your target, you are most likely going to hit it to the right.

I've had many discussions about eye alignment with my dear friend Dr. Craig Farnsworth, an optometrist-turned-golf guru who has successfully worked with famous golf pros from all over the world. The Doc teaches at The Palms Golf Club in La Quinta, Ca., where we're both members. We like to talk golf and share information.

Another day at the office for Doc Farnsworth and Venus!

Doc always starts his lessons with a vision test. This shows students where they think they are aiming their putts and where they're actually aiming. They can be two very different things.

Very rarely does anyone actually align the putter head squarely to their intended target. The position of our eyes won't allow it.

Here I use a putting triangle to show me where my club face is actually aimed.

It's not natural, and very rare, for humans to see an accurate putting line when looking straight down while the target is beyond the range of their vision. To see the target line you'd have to eyes in the side of your head or turn your head 45 degrees to see the target.

Imagine trying to walk down the street in this position. Or how about driving a car? Would you like to have heart surgery by a doctor who tilts their head to the side to get the right incision line? I DON'T THINK SO!

We have to accept that there is going to be a certain amount of visual distortion when putting. So, the first rule of putting is to find out where in the heck you are aiming!

Have a friend stand directly behind you at address and ask them where the putter is aimed. You may be surprised by the answer!

To check your own alignment, set your putter behind the ball, and then hold the putter in position and move behind the putter to look at how you've aligned. Betsy King used to do this all the time. She actually did this while playing in tournaments. It's not illegal, so why not try it?

This is the Betsy King method.

41

Dr. Farnsworth spends serious time giving golfers the correct feeling of how the eyes track the ball along the target line on the follow through. It is important that the eyes rotate along the target line with this precision stroke.

| Connect head and eye rotation, down target line. | Wrong head and eye rotation, left of target line. |

I think that putting along a chalk line or under a string aimed at the target are great visual aids for training your eyes to see a path that is truly square to the target line. Having the putter head pass under the string or along the chalk line will help you to see where your club face is aimed at address, impact, and at the finish position.

Putting under a string is a great visual aid for training your eyes.

Time for the Body Line

Once you learn to square your putter face to your target, then it's time to align the rest of your body to the target line.

The ultimate putting stroke is a pendulum-like, linear stroke. To create that stroke, it is most important that the shoulders are set squarely parallel to the target line. The only movement will be the rocking of the shoulders and arms under the head as the putter swings back and then forward through the ball.

Rock the shoulders back and then through along the target line.

43

If you find that your shoulders are aligned to the left of the target at address, which is a common offense, have a friend simply put their hand up against your back shoulder, and maintain slight pressure as you make your stroke. This square shoulder position will help you to keep the putter head along the correct target line. It will feel strange at first to keep that shoulder back and in a square position, but the results will turn you into a believer real fast!

I'll get by with a little help from my friend.

When it comes to positioning your feet at address, I go back to the **Venus View**: putting is personal.

I have seen every stance you can imagine, both open and closed and everything in between. I plead no contest. But I suggest if you are just starting in the game, a square stance parallel to the target line would be the easiest because it will also help you square the rest of your body to the same target line.

9

SAME OL'
SAME OL' ROUTINE

Every good golfer follows their own personal routine before each shot. Pre-shot routines aren't just habits or idiosyncrasies. Pre-shot routines are vitally important steps to get you out of your head (swing thoughts) and into your senses (feel).

When you're ready to putt, you can't be thinking about your line, the grain, the break, what's for dinner – anything! You have to feel as though you are on automatic pilot.

On the golf course you have to leave all thoughts about the mechanics of your stroke back on the practice green. You've worked on your mechanics; it's now time to "play" the game.

A simple, repeatable pre-putt routine will help you turn off your thoughts and turn you into a putting machine. Let me go through my pre-putt routine to give you a basis for developing your own.

The first thing I do is get a sense of how the surrounding land slopes as I walk to the green.

Get a sense for the break.

I start reading my putt while my playing partners are playing their own shots and putts. I look at my line from all sides of the cup.

Read your putt while others are playing their own shots.

When it's my turn to putt, I'm ready to go. I align my ball with the manufacturer's name lined up along my target line.

That way, I know the ball is aimed where I intend it to go. (If the logo on your favorite ball is curved or a symbol, you can mark a straight line on your ball with a felt pen and line up with that. A lot of pros do it.)

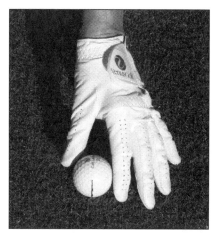

Use logo or line as an alignment aid.

Then, I walk behind the ball and take one final look to get a clear visualization of my intended line.

One final read before I address the ball.

I approach the ball and take my "V Factor" stance just short of the golf ball and take one practice stroke. I do this to loosen up and get a sense for how far back and forward I need to swing the putter for the distance I need.

A practice stroke is part of my routine.

The key to stroking a good putt is to start with your putter head square to your target line. When you're sure that the clubhead is properly aligned, then square your body to that line and assume your correct posture position.

Setting up clubface.

Setting feet, and taking correct posture position.

Once I'm in position, I rotate my head slightly along my target line — keeping my eyes parallel to that line — to get one last visual input of my intended putt. I look back down at the ball and focus on where I want to make solid contact on the ball. Then, I execute my stroke.

"ready"   "set"   "go"

10

READING LESSONS

The Venus Double D Putting Theory

The **Venus View** for putting is very simple:
- When you are stroking a long putt, the most important factor is Distance.
- When you are stroking a short putt, the most important factor is Direction

On long putts over 20 feet, distance is the key. The goal is to have the ball stop somewhere close to the hole. In golf language, that's a "lag" putt. If it goes in, that's a bonus.

Lags putts are about distance. Putt into a 3 foot circle around the hole.

On short putts direction is the key, so the putt can be struck more aggressively. The goal is to sink it. Because the most important factor is direction, it's easier to keep the ball on line if the putter follows through in an accelerating linear motion.

Short putts are about direction. Stroke the ball firmly on your target line.

Of the two D's, distance is the most important. Without a good sense for distance, it's hard to get the ball close to the cup. More strokes are wasted on the greens because the ball is hit too short or too far rather than off line.

Distance control is something you will need to invest time in if you want to take your game to the next level.

Noticing the Obvious

Every day I see golfers turning the simple act of reading a green into a science project. While accurately reading a green has as much to do with experience as anything else, basic human awareness should come into play before you even set foot on the putting surface.

As you approach the green take time to note where any mountains or hills are located or where there is a lake or ocean nearby. Putts are going to break away from mountains or hills and towards lower ground such as lakes or oceans.

If you are playing on a windy day, the wind will affect the way the ball will roll on the green. If you are putting into the wind, it will slow it down; if you are putting downwind, the ball is going to roll farther than usual. And in cross winds, the break on a putt will most likely be exaggerated in the direction the wind is blowing.

The more you play (and practice) the better you'll become at reading greens as you become more familiar with your home golf course, and start getting a "feel" for greens in general. By feel, I mean an acquired sense of how to play certain slopes, different speeds, and when the grain is strong enough to affect the roll of your ball.

55

Factor in elements such as the mountains, the water, and the wind.

Here comes that Grainy Day

Reading greens has enough variables without adding the reading of the grain. The "grain" is the direction the grass is growing. It doesn't grow straight up, but lies over in certain directions thus affecting the roll of the ball. Grain is most pronounced in Bermuda grasses used in warm climates. In cooler climates, bent grass is used for greens and it has little or no grain.

In trying to read Bermuda greens, I've found that I can tell which way the grain is going by walking up to the cup and looking down at the hole to see which way the grass is growing over the edge.

I know that if I'm putting into the grain, the ball is going to roll slower than it would normally and not roll as far. Conversely, if the grass is growing away from me, the ball is going to roll faster and further with the grain.

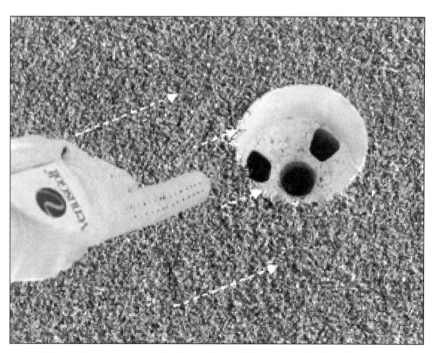

If grass is growing over the hole, the grain is growing in that direction.

Putting across the grain is going to affect the roll on the ball. The putt will roll in the direction that grass is growing. If you have a putt across a grain growing to your right, then it's a safe bet that you need to stroke the ball on a target line to the left, because the ball is most likely going to break more to the right than usual.

The ball will break more right when the grain is growing that direction.

Grain can be a real pain, but it is a fact of golf. So practice all you can, use your imagination, and don't let it beat you. Putt smart!

Taking A Better Look

I used to believe that the best "read" for every putt came from behind the ball looking directly to the cup. Perhaps it was because I was too lazy to walk around and actually scout out any other angles. I honestly believed that this was the best read anyone could make, and anything more was just complicating the process.

That was before I met my friend, Doc Farnsworth. He proved to me that there was in fact a more accurate way for me to read putts.

Although every angle should be examined, the most accurate read for me turned out to be looking at the putt from the hole back to my golf ball. You may find this to be true for you, too.

Don't be surprised if your most accurate read is from behind the hole back to the ball.

Making A Commitment

Committing to anything in life is not an easy thing to do, and putting is no different. To be a good putter, you must commit to your line, commit to your speed and then let it go.

Trust your read and your speed.

59

11

THE VENUS PICK SIX PUTTING TIPS

I have always been a big fan of CliffsNotes, and that's why I'm happy to give you the "VenusNotes" version of my six top putting tips.

1. Putt with Intent

Read your putt very carefully from all sides of the hole. Be very clear and specific about your line and the distance you want to hit it. Once you have programmed your mental computer with that data, commit to the putt and stroke the ball with every intention of sinking it!

Go in!

2. Give Me a "V"

Assume the "V Factor" position at address with your shoulders parallel to the target line. The elbows are relaxed and bent outward creating a V (which can be narrow or wide depending on your preference). Maintain the V throughout the putting stroke. Position your eyes directly over the ball and parallel to the target line.

Set up in the now famous "V Factor" position.

Eyes are directly over the ball.

3. Square Clubface at Impact

If the clubface is not square to your target line at impact the ball will not stay on your intended line. That's a simple rule of physics. If the heel of the putter is behind the toe, it is closed. If the heel is ahead of the toe, the putter face is open. If the face of the putter is perpendicular to the target line, the putter is square.

Open clubface.

Closed clubface.

Square clubface.

4. *Stroke On a Linear, Straight Path*

The most consistent stroke for putting is a straight line, back and through. Visualize a simple pendulum motion, in perfect rhythm going back and forth at the same pace and the same distance – along a linear path.

Rock your shoulders back and through along the target line.

5. *Solid Contact*

It is vital to put a good roll on the ball. Focus on making solid contact on the sweet spot of the putter, which is usually indicated with a line or alignment mark on the top of the clubhead.

Make solid contact against the line of your putter.

6. *Accelerate Through the Ball to Your Finish Position*

The putting stroke needs to be smooth from start to finish or the ball could roll off line and come up short of the hole. Exaggerate your stroke through the ball when you are practicing and bring that positive stroke to the golf course. Accelerate the clubhead through the stroke and hold your finish position.

Practice holding your finish.

12

CHIPPING

The chipping stroke is simply a longer version of the linear putting stroke. Both are accomplished using the "V Factor" setup, a pendulum stroke, and a sweeping tick-tock rhythm that ends in a balanced finish position.

When you practice your putting stroke, you are also practicing your chipping stroke. The **Venus View** is simple: Chipping is nothing more than putting with a lofted club.

Notice the same "V Factor" address positions with both putting and chipping.

Show Me the Money

The so-called "money club" in golf has always been the putter. After giving thousands of chipping lessons, I'm changing that.

If you really want to putt for "dough" and dramatically lower your scores, you first have to learn how to chip it close to the hole so you have a legitimate chance of making those "money" putts.

Decisions, Decisions

I know many of you like to use a different club for every lie and situation, like the better players do. I also know that this approach simply complicates chipping more than necessary, especially if you don't have the time to practice every day. Unless you have that time, I suggest you first become a master of one club.

Just like choosing a putter, selecting a favorite iron to chip with is personal. My favorite is an 8 iron, although I know many golfers prefer using a seven iron, a nine or pitching wedge.

Take your pick.

I also see many golfers who carry a "chipper" or some kind of club designed specifically for a low, running type shot. I think these utility clubs are not only a good idea, but the clubs of the future.

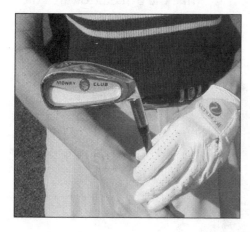

The Money Club™, a chipper with the loft of an 8 iron.

Making Magic

Before we get into the fundamentals of chipping, I want to take a close look at what I think is a very important chipping concept.

Let's take my favorite, the 8 iron. It's clearly not designed for putting. To use a chipping stroke that is similar to the putting stroke, you need to be creative to transform this 8 iron into a "great iron" for chipping.

It will take imagination to transform this 8 iron into a putting iron.

Place the club upright so that the toe portion is resting on the grass and the heel is raised slightly above the grass. Because the clubhead is resting on the toe, the new contact point is more towards the toe as well. You want to strike the ball out towards the toe of the clubface.

The new contact point is now outside of center, more on the toe.

By setting the clubhead this way, you will be able to assume your "V Factor" putting posture with your elbows relaxed outwards in a "V" and your eyes positioned directly over the ball. Grip down on the handle so you will feel as though you are actually putting.

This set up looks similar to a putting strip.

13

BACK TO
THE BASICS

Give Me Another "V"

By incorporating the "V Factor" in your address position you'll be ready to execute the pendulum chipping stroke.

The very act of placing the elbows in the shape of a "V" firms up the wrists and allows the arms and shoulders to work together as a unit. From this "V Factor" chipping position, place your eyes directly over the ball, and rock your shoulders gently back and forth as if you were "rocking the baby." That's it, it's that simple.

73

Back to the pendulum motion, keeping the V constant.

Getting a Grip to Chip

Your grip is of personal preference, but here are a few proven grip tips to improve your chipping.

Grip down on the handle of the club close to the shaft so whichever club you have decided to chip with will play and feel more like a putter.

Grip down on the handle for better control.

Although you can use a full swing grip for a chip, I personally use a putting grip. After all, a chip is like a putt so you need a grip that will firm up the hands and wrists.

I suggest that you position your hands on the club in the exact manner as you would your putter.

The palms of both hands should face each other with the fingers under the handle and the thumbs directly down the front of the shaft. If you like to putt lead hand low, then you can certainly chip that way too.

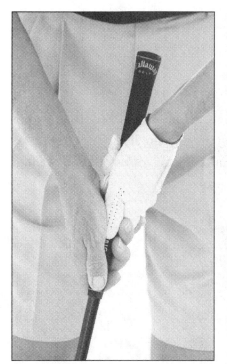

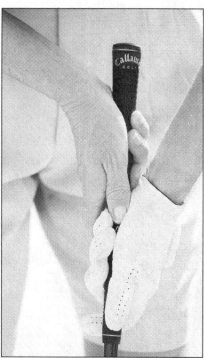

Use your putting grip for your chips.

A lead hand low grip is perfectly acceptable for chipping also.

The Stance

When you set up to chip, think to yourself that the club you're using "is" a putter and that you are setting up over a putt.

As I mentioned in the alignment portion on putting, foot position is personal. I have seen good players set up with both closed and open stances. I would certainly start out with a square stance to the target line if you are a beginner, because that will make it easier to line up your body parallel to your target line.

Chipping with square stance.

Because there is very little weight shift with a chip, there is no need for an extra wide stance. I set up with my feet comfortly positioned, shoulder width apart because that gives me a good feeling for the pendulum motion of the stroke.

No need for an extra wide stance because there is little weight shift.

Good Posture is a Must

Set up in the same posture when you putt. You are creating the identical pendulum putting motion, so don't change anything.

Chipping posture is the same as putting posture.

77

If you set up in a crouching type putting position, then that is how you should set up over your chips. If you like to stand tall over your putts, then that's your answer to the posture position.

Anchor Yourself

Like putting, chipping is a precision stroke so weight shift is kept to a minimum.

Once you have assumed your putting posture and your eyes are positioned directly over the ball, lean your weight slightly to your lead side. Shift enough weight to make you feel "anchored," just as you anchored yourself when putting.

Anchor's away!

Have someone push you gently with two fingers from all sides to make sure that you are balanced and truly "anchored."

Susan McCallum is not really "pushy," she is just being a good friend.

Ball Position Is Key

To ensure a descending blow and to make solid contact easier, position the ball just back of center in your stance.

Notice ball is back of center in stance.

Playing the ball back of center positions your hands slightly ahead of the ball (forward press) at address. This also makes it easier to make solid contact because the hands will be leading the clubface at impact.

Square the Clubface

Solid ball contact starts with a square clubface. The clubface has to return to a square position at impact for solid chips with true roll.

To make solid contact, keep the clubface square to the target line through the stroke.

Keep the clubface square and moving down the target line.

Swing Path

The swing path for chipping is the same linear path as for putting.

The swing path for chipping is the same linear path as for putting.

To encourage the club to trace on a straight path, the first and most important alignment step you can make is to square the clubface to the target line. Then, set your body parallel to that target line and get into your "V Factor" putting position.

Align clubface first.

Then align body to target line.

Because you are standing closer to the ball in the chipping address position than you would for a full swing, your eyes will be positioned directly over the ball and parallel with the target line.

Feel like you are putting your chip shot.

This putting-style set up position will make it easy for you to keep the club swinging straight back and straight through on a linear swing path.

The Rhythm Method for Chipping

The chipping motion is rhythmic, smooth back and smooth through. The "tick, tock" sound of a clock, or "beep, beep" sound of a metronome is a great swing key to simulate the pendulum tempo of a chip.

If counting or making up some kind of other sound helps to create a rhythm that builds a consistent chipping stroke, then by all means do it!

Finish what You've Started

Your finish position with a chip will be very similar to your finish position with a putt. On a chip, the clubhead will finish on a higher arc because it was a longer stroke.

Stay in the "tilt" posture position with your upper body that you assumed at address. Resist the temptation to lift up your head and admire your shot as you swing through the ball. Hold your finish position until the stroke is completed.

Pose like a pro and stay in your tilt position as you hold your finish.

Taylor's Question

Speaking of posing, I am pleased to introduce one of my favorite students, eleven year old Taylor Manning.

As you can see, Taylor has long hair, rosy cheeks and a big smile that greets me with every lesson. If you ask Taylor how she's doing, she will eagerly reply: "Life is good!" This is the child we all wish we had!

*Junior Venus,
Taylor Manning,
striking a pose.*

Children are wonderful students because they are not afraid to ask questions. And as every parent knows, they ask a lot of them.

Taylor has posed some great ones, and came up with a gem on chipping.

She asked: "How far back from the green can I still use my 'V Factor' chip, and when do I switch to a 'Y Factor' pitch?"

The **Venus View** is simple: The golf ball has no clue what club you use or technique you use to hit it. There is no wrong or right answer.

It's a personal choice which shot you hit and something that you'll learn through practice and experimentation.

I personally use the linear chipping motion as far back as 10 to 15 yards off the green.

I chip from that distance whenever the situation permits because it is an easier stroke to control. A pitch shot requires more wrist action and therefore is a more complicated motion. Chipping is simpler than pitching, so there's a better chance of getting the ball close to the hole.

As long as I have a good lie with no deep grass or trouble in front of my golf ball, and there's room to roll the ball on the green, I will chip.

But if I need height on the shot to clear trouble ahead, or need to put added spin on the ball to get it to stop on the green, then chipping is no longer an option. Then it's time to hit a pitch shot, no matter how close I am to the green.

I choose to chip when I can.

I pitch when I need to get the ball into the air and over trouble.

Taylor is the model of perfection on these two shots, in fact she looks like a model, so let's use Taylor to model for us the differences between the "Y Factor" set up for ground strokes and the "V Factor" set up for air strokes.

The "V Factor" address position for chipping.

The "Y Factor" address position for pitching.

Thank you Taylor, I could not have found a better model. By the way, you are right, "Life is Good!"

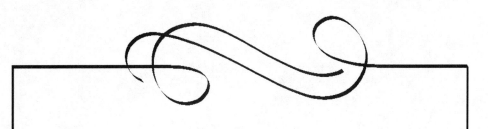

PART 2

AIR SHOTS

Pitching, Sand & Lob

1

THE VENUS
PITCH

A pitch shot is just that, a pitch, much like tossing a softball underhand. In essence, the pitching motion is a mini version of the full swing.

You can use a pitch shot anywhere from a few feet off the green, to 40 or 50 yards out in the fairway. The reason you are pitching in the first place is to get the ball airborne so that it will carry to the green.

Although a pitching wedge is included in every set of clubs, I would suggest that you use a sand wedge (56 degrees loft, on average) or even a lob wedge (60 degrees) to pitch with. Both clubs have more loft than the pitching wedge and that makes it easier to stop the ball because the golf ball will fly high off the clubface.

L-wedge on left --
Sand wedge on right.

The Basic Golf Grip

Whatever grip style you use for your full swing is the grip to use for pitching. Here are the three basic grips:

The ten finger grip is popular among beginners and is a wonderful grip for short shots because it allows all your fingers and both thumbs to be on the handle of the club. This will give you better control and more "feel" for the short shots.

The ten finger grip.

The overlapping or Vardon grip is the most popular grip among tour pros and amateurs. It's similar to the ten finger grip but with the pinky finger of the bottom hand resting snugly between the first and second fingers of the bottom hand.

The overlapping grip

The interlocking grip refers to the interlocking of the two pinky fingers. Jack Nicklaus uses it, so does Tiger. I don't recommend it to my women golfers because it is not comfortable, but it's still a popular grip among stronger players.

The interlocking grip

Whichever grip you choose, it is important that it gives you a comfortable hold on the club and allows your wrists and hands to be flexible, not rigid. Your wrists will hinge slightly on the backswing so your grip has to allow for movement in your hands and wrists.

Notice how wrists hinge.

Taking A Stance

Pitch shots are not full shots, so you don't have to take a wide stance. Set your feet apart so that you are comfortable, but not so wide apart that you will be tempted to make a big weight shift. You will use your legs slightly with a pitch shot, just as you would if you were tossing a ball. Keep the movement to a minimum with the emphasis on making solid ball contact.

Maintain a comfortable stance.

You will also want to set up in your "tossing" or "open" position. That means that your lead foot is slightly back from the target line and the toe is pointed slightly outwards. Pitching is pitching, whether it's a golf ball or a softball. The "open" stance will allow you to follow through and turn your hips towards your target.

Pitching is similar to an underhand toss.

Posture Perfect

Your posture over a pitch shot will depend on how tall you are. I'm not very tall at 5 ft. 3 in., so I don't set up with a lot of forward tilt in my spine. My friend Steve Adams, who is 6 ft. 4 in. looks stooped over the ball compared to me. At address, as in the full swing, you want to feel balanced. It's an athletic position with knees slightly flexed and your weight on the balls of your feet.

Notice how tall at address Venus looks compared to Steve, yet our clubs are in identical position.

Give Me a "Y"

If you have read my first book, Venus On The Fairway, then you know that I'm a strong believer in the importance of the "Y Factor" in the full-swing address position.

The "Y" I'm talking about is the shape your arms and the club form when you set up to the ball at address position.

The "Y Factor" set up position.

This is the starting point for all full swing and pitch shots. Give me a Y at address because that is exactly what your arms and the club will form at the all important moment of truth — impact.

Back to the "Y Factor" at impact.

Sandra Post On Ball Position

I have played with a lot of pros in my day, but few could scramble in the league of my friend Sandra Post, still the youngest player to win an LPGA Major tournament.

Still friends after all these years.

95

When the fun-loving Canadian was winning on the LPGA tour, she was one of the best!

Not surprisingly, Sandra is now a very successful golf instructor in Canada with her teaching academy in Caledon, Ontario. You can tell by her enthusiasm that she just loves what she does. I particularly love the way she teaches ball position for pitching, so much so that I'm stealing it for this book!

It's okay, I told her I would.

What Sandra does is she puts a big letter R on the right shoe of her students and a big L on the left shoe (the opposite for left-handers). She then explains that the R stands for "roll" and the L stands for "loft".

If you want to hit a lower, rolling shot, position the ball back toward your R foot.

If you want to hit a higher, lofted shot, position the ball toward your L foot.

"R" is for roll.

"L" is for loft.

If you are just starting out, I recommend that you play the ball in the middle of your stance until you can master solid ball contact. Once you feel that you're making good contact, start experimenting by positioning the ball back and then forward in your stance. See how the different ball positions will affect the ball flight of your pitches, creating rolling and lofted shots.

Have fun with it, learn from Sandra and use your imagination.

Visualization

Speaking of imagination, you need a clear mental image of your target if you are going to be good at the pitch shot. It really helps to visualize the spot you want the ball to land. Imagine you are tossing a ball to that spot.

I see my target.

Also picture in your mind how high the ball is going to fly. Picking a height, or loft, is as important as picking a landing spot.

My target just got a lot taller

Getting Started

I know it's not easy to get the swing started from a dead stand still. The only way to get it all started is to keep the club in motion as much as possible before you pull the trigger.

Having a "waggle" will help. The "waggle" is a way to keep the arms and hands relaxed by waving or waggling the club back and forth above the ball as you settle in to the shot. Waggle the club a few times at address to keep yourself loose before you start the club away.

Let the club waggle forward and back.

Take a couple of mini practice swings while you study your shot and visualize your target area. The last thing you want to do is freeze over the ball. The muscles in your forearms and shoulders will tighten and you won't be able to make a free flowing swing.

Backswing in Motion

How far back you take the club on your backswing will depend on how far you want to hit your shot. You will need to put in some practice time to know just how far you hit the ball with different backswings.

Shoulder high backswing.

But remember, match the length of your backswing with the length of your follow through. That pendulum just keeps on swinging.

Shoulder-high follow through.

99

Venus Pitching Fundamental 101

The key to pitching the golf ball with any kind of success and consistency is to keep your lead wrist flat at impact! The left wrist does not assist in hitting the golf ball, and this may be the most valuable golf tip of all!

This could be the epiphany you were hoping for when you bought this book. Underline this next paragraph and highlight it with a magic marker.

The **Venus View** on pitching is: "The clubhead does not lead the hands at impact. The hands lead the clubhead at impact."

When the clubhead passes the hands at impact, the wrists have cupped and you will most likely hit a flip or scoop shot!

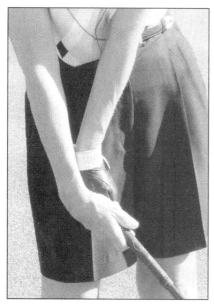 

You do not want your hands to hinge at impact.
This is cupped and I cannot even stand to look at these pictures!

When the hands lead the clubhead at impact, the lead wrist does not hinge. It stays flat. That position of the lead wrist at impact is what is considered to be "against it," "solid," or just plain "pure!"

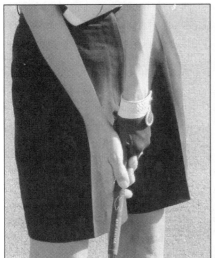 

You want your hands to lead the clubface at impact. This is "pure."

Following Through

I mentioned that pitching is the same motion as tossing a ball underhand, so your finish position should be the same for this shot also.

Your body will be facing the target when you toss a softball, so your body should be facing the target after you have finished pitching a golf ball.

"Pitch" your pitch shots.

Your entire body rotates toward the target on the follow through while maintaining the tilt position that you assumed in your set up. The hips rotate too, and you finish in a balanced stance when the swing is completed.

You know you have finished the swing correctly when your belt buckle is facing the target. Hold that pose and watch where the ball lands so you can get feedback for the next time.

I will constantly be working on my balance.

Smoothing Out Those Up's and Downs

You can always expect those skill-testing uphill and downhill lies around the greens when you're playing golf. The game would be boring without the challenge of a few ups and downs.

The thing to remember on these shots is to keep your shoulders as parallel to the slope as possible. This will be much easier on uphill lies because your shoulders are already slightly tilted thanks to your back hand being lower on the grip of the club to start with.

Uphill shots are also easier because the slope will assist you in hitting the ball up into the air. Higher shots will stop more quickly on the green. But make sure you hit the ball hard enough to reach your desired distance from an uphill lie. It's often very easy to hit the ball so high that it spends all of its energy in the air and doesn't go as far as you wanted.

Natural shoulder tilt with uphill lie.

Downhill slopes are another story. When pitching from a downhill lie you need to pay attention. Tilt your shoulders downward to parallel the ground as much as possible. It won't feel natural, but you must do it because you want to swing as much on the plane of the downhill slope as you physically can. It will help to take a practice swing with this shot.

Unnatural shoulder tilt with downhill lie.

I start my students to play both shots in the middle of their stance. Until you are more experienced, I would suggest you do the same. Solid ball contact is absolutely crucial to the success of uphill and downhill shots.

Getting fancy with ball positions is great if you practice a lot and have a lot of confidence. In the meantime, play the percentages and pitch the shot toward the green from the middle of your stance. That way, it's more likely that you'll be making your next shot with a putter.

Hit and Stop -
For Advanced Golfers Only

Don't you just love to watch a pro hit a pitch shot that takes one hop and stops immediately? It's fun to watch but even more fun to do it yourself!

The stance for the hit and stop shot is slightly open, with the ball positioned back from the center of the stance. Your hands have to be well in front of the ball at address, with the clubface square, not open, to the target.

Setting up for the hit and stop. Ball back, hands forward.

105

Grip the club more firmly than usual with both hands for added control, and imagine that they will be stiffer than normal throughout the swing. This is not a shot that can tolerate flippy wrists or hands.

Take your wedge of choice back in a fairly short but upright arc. Then, hit a descending blow that travels down and through the ball.

The key is to stop, or restrict, your follow through just beyond impact. It's this abrupt stopping action that puts all the backspin on the ball.

Red light, put on the brakes!

With practice, you will fly the ball almost to the flagstick, then-watch it "dance" after one hop. Once you master this shot, you will be dancing too!

Shank You Very Much!

I hate to even bring this shot up, but inquiring minds always want to know what went wrong to cause a shank? Too often on pitch shots, golfers start the club back by rolling the clubface open almost immediately. By opening the clubface so early in the swing, the swing path suddenly is sharply to the inside. That means nothing but trouble on the downswing.

Clubface too open and inside on backswing.

"Ouch"

The clubhead will return on a severe inside path and because it has to swing out to return to the ball, it can result in the dreaded "shank." (Gulp!) The hosel – where the clubhead joins the shaft — strikes the ball and sends it rocketing off at a right angle to the intended target line. Much chaos and confusion follows, often accompanied by inventive use of language.

To avoid that dreaded shot, make sure you sweep the club away squarely from the ball on the backswing. Don't fan the clubface open on your takeaway!

Square take away.   *Solid contact.*

I realize nobody wants to experience, let alone witness, such an ugly shot. But hopefully you will "thank me very much" for explaining what in the world goes wrong when it does happen.

HOW TO BE A
SAND SHARK

Just the thought of a ball landing in a sand trap can be the cause of golf's ultimate fear factor. But it shouldn't be that way! Sand traps can be easily tamed and even mastered with a few basic Venus fundamentals. Sand traps should in fact be a golf shot that is fun and welcomed.

One of the reasons why is that unlike other short game shots, you don't have to be as precise in sand as on grass. The clubface is striking the sand behind the ball, not the ball itself. You can hit anywhere from one to three inches behind the ball and still get a great result. So what's to be afraid of?

Sand shots can actually be fun.

Lob or Sand Wedge

When I was competing on tour it was rare for anyone to consider hitting anything but a sand wedge out of a greenside bunker. Today I advise everyone to practice using both the sand (56 degrees loft) and the lob or L wedge (60 degrees). Try them both and compare how high and far you can carry the ball with each because not all bunkers shots are equal.

Just love my sand and lob wedge!

If you have a standard greenside sand shot with not too high of a 'lip' or edge to get over, and a fair amount of green between you and the pin, use your sand wedge.

Using a sand wedge.

If you're in a greenside bunker with a high lip that you have to carry your golf ball over, then definitely use your lob wedge.

Using a lob wedge.

The Sound Of Music

I would like to share the most unique bunker tip I have ever "heard." I learned it many years ago from my mentor, the late golfing legend Johnny Revolta and I promised him that I would pass it on.

Johnny told me that a good sand shot has a particular sound to it, which we will call a "thud." I love to tell my students, "If you don't hear a "thud," it's probably a "dud!"

Name that tune!

The thud sound is achieved when the sole, or bottom edge, of the clubhead bounces aggressively into the sand behind the ball and accelerates through the ball. If you sweep the ball, stop at the ball, or dig into the back of the ball, you can't make the sound that's music to a bunker player's ear — "thud."

Once you tune in to that sound, you're on your way to good bunker play.

Start With A Weak Grip

Weaken your grip from the start to avoid a low driving shot that will get you into nothing but more trouble.

You want to get the ball in the air out of bunkers and control how far it will roll. The last thing you want to do is rotate your hands into a "strong" grip position at impact which closes the clubface and causes a low shot.

Be sure to check your hands in the sand, because strong is wrong!

A grip is "strong" if the top or lead hand is rotated away from the target line so that the knuckles rather than the back of the hand are facing the target.

112

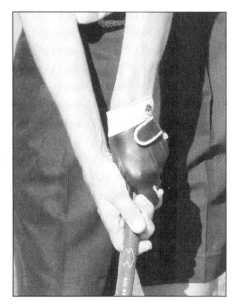

A strong grip.

In the sand, you want a weak or neutral grip at address.

Adjust the top hand more under the handle of the club so the back of that hand is facing the target. Your thumb should be straight down the front of the handle and you will be able to see only one knuckle, not two or three.

A weak grip.

With a weaker grip, the clubface will stay in the correct position and you'll have a tough time closing it coming through the ball.

Clubface stays open.

Open Stance

Just like the pitch shot, the sand shot is similar to an underhand pitching motion. Visualize tossing a softball underhand onto the green. To execute the shot you need to set up in your "tossing stance" with your body "open" to your target.

An open stance is a tossing stance.

Go Outside to Get In

From the open stance position, the goal is to swing the club back along the foot line on a more upright plane than a standard fairway pitch shot. This steeper plane creates the leverage needed to bounce the sole of the wedge into the sand with a "thud" and send the ball high into the air. If your swing plane is too flat and low, you won't hear the thud and you'll risk "blading" the ball, hitting it with the leading edge of the clubface.

The arc of the sand shot swing is actually so steep that the swing path is from the outside to in. If I were tracing that path, a line would show the club swinging back and up outside the target line, then returning inside of the target line.

This outside-to-in swing path creates a tremendous amount of leverage which helps to get the ball up and out of the sand. It also creates side spin on the ball which helps to stop the ball on the green.

Hinge your wrists at the top.

Start away to the outside,

Swing down to the inside.

Finish facing your target.

Open for Business

Begin with an open clubface – so the sole of the club will bounce into the sand rather than dig into it. By opening the clubface at address you increase the loft of the club and the amount of bounce of the sole.

Avoid squaring clubface.

Keep clubface open.

Be sure you keep the clubface open when you strike behind the ball so that the sole of the club will do its job. Let it bounce, not dig in, and make that beautiful "thud" sound.

Ball Position

Sand shots need higher trajectory, so position the ball forward in your stance: just inside your left instep at address.

This will promote a higher shot, and also encourage the club-head to hit behind the ball and slide easily through the sand. It will also position your head well behind the ball, which will help you stay behind the ball at impact.

Room for Error

You don't need to hit the ball perfectly — you just have to hit one to three inches behind the ball. The sole of the sand wedge is designed to guide the wedge through the sand and under the ball, sending the golf ball up and on its way with a lot of backspin.

Fillet of "Sole".

Going to the Cleaners — Spin and Fold

Here is a two-step sand shot tip that I know you have never heard in your life because I made it up. I also know it works because I use it myself!

Step one: Clear your hips as you follow through. If your hips do not clear fast enough on the downswing, then the clubhead will swing too steeply downward and dig into the sand like a regular golf shot, instead of bouncing off the sand with a thud.

To help you visualize clearing your hips, imagine someone has their finger in your lead pocket and is pulling your hips open so that your belt buckle is facing the target when you follow through. You need to "spin" to get to step two.

Imagine someone is spinning your hips open with their finger.

Step two: Fold your lead elbow up on the follow through. This is one of the most overlooked secrets to great sand play.

The lead elbow cannot be rigid on the follow through. It must fold upward after impact. It is this upward motion of the elbow that sends the ball upwards.

The quicker the folding motion, the higher and shorter the ball will fly.

Fold your elbow.

Next time you are in the sand just think "spin" and "fold" and you'll be taking your friends to the cleaners!

Spin and fold.

The Short and Long of It

Practice sand shots of different lengths with your spin and fold method. For short sand shots, fold the lead elbow quickly to take a short divot.

On medium length shots, take a medium length divot. And for long sand shots, swing through the ball as though you are making a swing on the fairway letting your lead elbow swing on out through to the finish.

You can take a divot a foot long for a long bunker shot. Practice and see how you can control the distance of the shot by controlling the length of your divots.

Divot control.

Fried Eggs

You don't have to be a "ham" to handle a "fried egg." Golfers call a buried lie in a bunker a fried egg because the ball looks like the yolk and the surrounding sand like the white of a fried egg. It's a tough shot but there are ways to get yourself out of the frying pan and on to the green.

A fried egg.

Start by opening your stance, and placing your hands in their "Y" position so that your hands are ahead of the ball at address. Swing your sand or L wedge back as steeply as possible to be able to swing down on a sharp angle.

Start in your "Y" position so you can swing downward behind the ball.

Aim for a spot about two inches behind the ball and hit down on that spot. Swing hard, deep and hope for a little luck.

The #1 objective is to get out.

Forget about a follow through from a fried egg lie. The steep arc of this shot and the sand will stop the clubhead preventing any follow through. The ball will not have much backspin, so plan on extra roll. (Nothing better than an extra roll with a fried egg!)

Lies, Lies And More Lies

There's no guarantee of a level lie in a bunker, in fact some are downright awkward. Uphill and downhill lies are all too common in greenside bunkers.

The key to is to swing with the shape of the slope.

Uphill lie: As with shots from slopes in the fairway, set up with your shoulders tilted with the slope.

Exaggerate your tilt so you can swing along the upward slope. Play the ball in the middle of your stance and factor in that the ball is going to come out extra high, so hit the ball a bit harder to carry it to your target.

Tilt your shoulders with the slope.

Downhill lie: This is a very tough shot because the natural shoulder tilt promotes an upward swing while you need a downward swing for this shot.

To execute this shot successfully tilt your shoulders as much as possible with the downhill slope. This is not as easy as the uphill lie and your shoulders will not actually tilt downward.

Do the best you can to tilt your shoulders down with the slope.

123

Position the ball in the middle of your stance and make your best effort to swing down along with the slope. Resist the temptation to swing up, and keep the clubhead swinging deep into the sand so that you do not hit the ball thin and send it screaming out of the bunker across the green.

A Positive Spin

A positive attitude may be the key ingredient to becoming a sand shark in the bunkers. Pick a spot you want the ball to land and imagine the ball flying high in the air and landing on your intended spot.

You have the FUNdamentals, so enjoy the challenge and don't let yourself get down or frustrated over a single bad bunker shot. We all know you are doing your best, so whatever the outcome "don't be a sand crab!"

Give it your best effort and accept the outcome.

I'm out, let's do lunch.

3

MASTERING THE LOB SHOT

The lob shot is a "must shot" for the design of today's golf courses. Many modern greens are elevated, fast, with severe slopes that allow little room for error. They require a shot that comes almost straight down and stops.

It's a high-risk shot if you don't practice it, but it's a shot you must have in your arsenal. Other than the fact that it's played off the grass, the lob shot technique is almost identical to a sand shot.

I use my 60 degree lob wedge for this short but high trajectory shot.

A lob shot is a fun shot, but it takes a lot of practice.

Taking the Gamble

Unlike the sand shot, with the lob shot you don't have the luxury of hitting a couple of inches behind the ball. If the lie is not right, the shot could end up a disaster.

A ball sitting on hard dirt or sitting down in high grass (a tight lie) are not good spots for a lob shot.

Too skinny!   *Too fat!*

The best surface to hit your lob shot from is a clean or fluffy lie where the ground is soft enough under the ball so the L wedge can easily slide under the ball.

Just right!

Open Sesame

To execute the lob shot, let's get back to basics. Set the clubface open to the target line to give the clubhead added loft. The clubhead is basically sitting on the bottom portion of the club, called the sole. The intention is to slide the sole under the ball at impact without closing the clubface.

Open your lead foot to the target line to get into your 'tossing the softball' position just like the sand shot set up. In fact, you can pretend you are hitting out of the sand.

Open your stance, open your clubface, and give it your sand shot swing.

129

Grip of the "Weak"

Adjust your lead hand on the grip so the back of your hand is facing the target. Your thumb should be straight down the front of the club and you will see only one knuckle on your lead or top hand at address position. You are looking for extra height, not distance with a lob shot.

Lead hand needs to be in a "weak" position for a lob shot.

130

Sandra on Ball Position

Let's go back to what Sandra Post taught us about ball position. If you want to hit the ball with loft, then position the ball off your lead foot. That is where you will play a lob shot because if ever there was a time to hit it with loft, it's now!

Back to "L" for loft.

Backswing in Motion

You want the arc of your backswing to be steep so you can achieve the leverage needed to hit downward behind the ball and drive the ball up into the air. One way to achieve such a steep arc is to hinge your wrists on the backswing so they will assist in getting the clubhead high.

Let your wrists hinge for leverage.

Back to the Cleaners

Just like the sand shot, spin your hips to the target as you swing down through impact. Then fold your lead elbow upwards as you swing on through to your finish position. Don't be a slob with your lob!

You can spin and fold for your lob shots too!

Pose for the Cameras

I realize that this may make you may feel like a real showboat, but hold your finish position when you've completed your swing.

Stay in your tilt position and watch the ball fly high and towards your target. Hold that finish for at least 2 to 3 seconds, just enough time for someone to take a picture when the ball lands close to the pin.

By holding that pose, you are creating muscle memory of a solid swing and improving your balance. You will need both to master the lob shot.

Just call me the "lob-ster."

PART 3

SHORT GAME DRILLS

VENUS DRILLS FOR BETTER SKILLS

To encourage you to practice the skills that will dramatically improve your game, I'd like to share some effective drills that will turn your practice into fun.

1. Putting

Tennis Ball Drill

Stroke short putts with a tennis ball instead of a golf ball to better your confidence. When you putt the much bigger tennis ball, the golf hole will look that much smaller. After hitting enough "sets" with a tennis ball, the hole will look like a bathtub when you resume hitting putts with a golf ball!

Venus practicing her forehand putt.

The Venus 2-Ball Drill

Place two golf balls on the practice green touching each other. Line them up squarely against your putter face.

Make your normal putting stroke, hitting both balls at the same time and see how far each ball rolls.

Practice hitting both balls at the same time.

You will get instant feedback. If the ball closest to the toe of the putter rolls farther than the other one, then you are closing the putter face at impact. If the ball closest to the heel of the putter rolls farther, that tells you that you are opening the putter face at impact.

When you can roll both balls the same distance, you know for certain that your putter face is square at impact.

I obviously hit this putt with the toe portion first.

Eyes Wide Shut Drill

Set up over a short putt on the practice green, make your read, and when you're ready to go, close your eyes.

Putting with your eyes closed will give a better "feel" for the distance you are stroking your putts. And, by taking the visual component out of the equation, you won't have the impulse to look up to see where the ball is going.

Close your eyes, and listen for the ball to hit the bottom of the cup.

"Ninja Venus"

Eyes on the Hole Drill

Now open your eyes and keep them open. And this time, don't look at the ball but look at the hole.

Stroke putts from 10 feet and closer while looking directly at the hole. It's the same concept as a basketball player looking at the basket instead of the ball when making a free throw.

By looking at the hole, you exaggerate the positive feeling of letting the putter head follow through to the hole.

I just love watching the ball go into the hole.

Two-Club Drill

Place two clubs on the green parallel to each other with just enough space in between to fit your putter head.

Sweep the clubhead back and though between the two clubs to make sure you are putting with a linear straight back and straight through stroke.

This is similar to using a putting track on the green.

Putt On Down the Line Drill

The ball rolls end-over-end on a good putt. When you see that end-over-end roll it gives you positive feedback that you hit the ball solidly on the sweet spot of the putter with the clubhead traveling on a straight back, straight through path.

To make it easier to see that true roll, practice putting with range balls that have lines around their equator, or with a ball which you've drawn a straight line around. Putt on down the line. The roll will let you known how well you are stroking it.

Practice with a line around the ball so you can check end over end roll.

Drinking Glass Drill

Joanne Carner taught me this drill years ago in Orlando, Florida when I was still competing on the LPGA Tour.

Always an aggressive putter herself, Joanne is a strong believer in stroking the ball to the back of the cup on short putts.

Her drill for this philosophy is to practice stroking putts into a typical drinking glass. This drill is unique because you can practice this one in your own home.

This drill always makes me thirsty!

142

Place a drinking glass on the carpet anywhere that you have a backstop for the glass, then stroke the ball hard enough to hit the back of the cup. You will definitely become more aggressive with your short putts, and you'll want to thank Joanne for her help!

Against a Board Drill

I like to practice my putting stroke by sweeping the putter head back and forth along a straight wooden board to get the feeling for a linear swing path.

You can also improvise with a flagstick on the golf course while you're waiting for your partners to putt out if you like. In fact, use any straight surface to groove your linear, straight back/straight through stroke.

143

Practice against a board ...   *or a flagstick.*

Under the String Drill

It is well worth the money to purchase a putting string so you can practice stroking putts along the correct target line.

The string gives you great and instant feedback. You'll know immediately if you are aimed on the actual target line and if your putter head is square to the target. Often times what we think is square to the hole, is not even close.

Putting under a string or a straight line is a great way to get visual feedback.

Metronome Drill

Get yourself a metronome to practice your tempo. Set the speed of the metronome to match your stroke. Then practice by yourself somewhere on the green and memorize that rhythm as though it were a dance step.

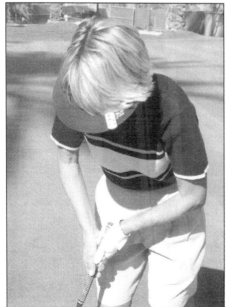

Putt to the beat.

2. Chipping

Get a Line Drill

A chip shot is a putt with loft, so the end-over-end roll is going to be just as important in chipping as it is in putting. Practice with a range ball that has a line around the equator or a ball that you've drawn a line around just as you did with the putter.

Make the shot and carefully watch the roll of the ball. The line on the ball should spin end-over-end when you stroke with a linear shaped chipping stroke.

Get a "line" on your chips.

145

Chip to a Coin Drill

To improve your focus and visualization, place a coin on the green where you want your chip shot to land, before it starts to roll towards the hole.

With practice, you eventually won't need anything on the green to help you 'see' exactly where you want the ball to land.

Chipping for money.

Three-foot Circle Drill

Stick golf tees in the practice green to form a three-foot circle around the hole. Practice chipping balls into that circle.

To expect to knock the ball into the cup every time is unrealistic, but chipping into a three-foot circle is realistic.

This is a good drill to hone your accuracy and instill confidence because you should be able to make that three-foot putt.

Use golf tees to imagine you are chipping into a 3 foot circle.

3. Pitching

Underhand Toss Drill

Toss the golf ball underhand a few times onto the green to get the feeling for how the throwing hand releases the ball and how the arm actually swings back and through during a pitch shot.

Toss the ball to feel the motion.

147

One-Arm Drill

Using the same hand you toss the ball with, grip your wedge and make that smooth tossing motion while striking the ball with one arm only.

You don't need to make a big swing with this drill, just get the tossing feeling.

The club will seem a bit heavy, so don't attempt long pitches with this drill. Just hit short shots to get the feeling of how your arm folds on the back swing and then unfolds on the follow through.

With this drill, you'll remember this feeling when you use both hands and make your normal pitch shots.

Club on the Green Drill

It's very important to practice with a purpose, and this drill is a perfect example.

Place a club on the practice green as a target. Practice pitching the ball just over the club and observe the ball as it rolls toward the hole.

148

You will need an extra club for this drill (to place on the green).

4. Sand

Into the Bucket Drill

Buckets are fun to hit balls into. So, when practicing your sand shots, grab a bucket and put it on the green. See how many balls you can land in it. This is not only fun, but an easy way to vary the length of shot you're practicing.

Eventually, when you get into a greenside bunker during a round, you will imagine a big bucket on the green and be confident that you can land the ball into your imaginary bucket.

Buckets make a great visual target.

149

Drawing a Line in the Sand Drill

In a normal round of golf, it is illegal to touch the sand before you hit your shot. A sand trap or bunker is deemed to be a "hazard" in the rules of the game. You cannot ground your club in any hazard on the course, and that includes the sand.

But when you're practicing, the rules don't apply. So go ahead and draw a line in the sand with your finger about two inches behind the ball. That's your target, not the ball.

Make your stand, draw a line in the sand.

Swing into the sand and see for yourself where you are making impact behind the ball. Feedback is important when you are practicing, and this is one way to get the feedback you need to make adjustments.

Tee it up Drill

To improve the swing path of your bunker shots, place a tee under the ball in the sand. This will prevent you from swinging too deeply. You want to avoid a "dud" and hear that magical "thud!"

Place a tee under the ball.

"Thud" the tee out from under the ball at impact.

151

<u>5. Lob</u>

Back To The Bucket Drill

The lob is a high trajectory shot that comes almost straight down, so you need an appropriate practice target. I personally love hitting balls into buckets, so here we go again.

Place any size bucket on the green and see how many balls you can lob into it. Don't be surprised if your friends want to join you. It's a fun drill and everybody gets a kick out of landing one in a bucket.

Don't kick the bucket, you need it to practice your lobs.

Up and Over Drill

Find any obstacle that will force you to get the ball up high and quickly. I used to hit balls over golf carts when I was really good.

Now, I'm afraid I may do some damage, so I have moved on to tree limbs and in this case, a ladder. This drill will help you learn to get the ball up high into the air and to do it quickly – with as little collateral damage as possible.

Step up to the challenge and find an obstacle that will force you to hit the ball extra high.

Over the Bunker Drill

This is more than just a drill. You'll need this particular shot many times when playing golf, so you might as well practice it as much as possible.

When you miss a green with your approach shot, so often you end up with a bunker between you and the hole.

This lob shot over a bunker requires you to fly the ball far enough to clear the bunker and high enough that you can stop the ball on the green.

With the over the bunker drill, distance is just as important as height.

Unless you really love the beach, practice lofting the ball safely onto the green.

153

And finally, **The Venus #1 Golf Drill: The Fun Factor!"**

   Make it a habit to smile, laugh, and enjoy the surroundings. Golf is the great escape, so take advantage of the moment and give thanks. Be kind to yourself and be kind to others. Learn to celebrate the good shots and put the "Fun Factor" back into your game. With enough practice having fun, the game of golf will no longer be about your "score," but a whole lot "more!"

Venus shows why we all play golf in the first place, The "Fun Factor!"

AFTERWORD

As with my first publication, "Venus On The Fairway," this has been a labor of love.

Venus On The Fringe was always intended to be:

A short book

About the short game

Written by a short woman

Mission Accomplished!

Dethin St...
AKA
"Venus"

VENUS VALUES

If you'd like more information on a wide range of Venus Golf products call 888-67VENUS, or visit the Venus website at www.venusgolf.com You will also find all you need to know about Venus products, golf schools, clinics, guest speaking services and Venus herself.

Now that you've seen some of my favorite training aids in *Venus on the Fringe*, here's how to get your own putting boards, putting strings, the putting tracks, and other fine training products. Contact Golf Around the World, Inc. by calling 1-800-824-4279 or by visiting www.golfaroundtheworld.com.

To order short game training aids including alignment guides, mirrors, lasers, or metronomes that fasten to your cap or visor, contact Eyeline Golf by calling 800-969-3764 or by visiting www.eyelinegolf.com.

When making purchases at Golf Around the World and Eyeline Golf use the code word "Venus" and receive a 10 percent discount on all your orders.

Take advantage of these Venus Values to have fun and improve you game.